Psychedelic Meadow

Selected Publications by Jeremy Reed

Poetry
The Isthmus of Samuel Greenberg (1976; 2nd edition 2018*)
Bleecker Street (1980)
By the Fisheries (1984)
Nero (1985)
Selected Poems (1987)
Engaging Form (1988)
Nineties (1990)
Red Haired Android (1992)
Kicks (1994)
Pop Stars, with Mick Rock (1995)
Sweet Sister Lyric (1996)
Saint Billie (2000)
Patron Saint of Eyeliner (2000)
Heartbreak Hotel (2002)
Duck and Sally Inside (2006)
Orange Sunshine (2006)
This Is How You Disappear (2007)
West End Survival Kit (2009)
Bona Drag (2009)*
Black Russian: Out-takes from the Airmen's Club 1978-9 (2010)
Piccadilly Bongo (with Marc Almond) (2010)
Bona Vada (2011)*
Whitehall Jackals (with Chris McCabe) (2013)
The Glamour Poet... (2014)*
Sooner or Later Frank (2014)
Shakespeare in Soho (2017)

Novels
The Lipstick Boys (1984)
Blue Rock (1987)
Red Eclipse (1989)
Inhabiting Shadows (1990)
Isidore (1991)
When The Whip Comes Down (1992)
Chasing Black Rainbows (1994)
The Pleasure Chateau (1994)
Diamond Nebula (1995)
Red Hot Lipstick (1996)
Sister Midnight (1997)
Dorian (1998)
Boy Caesar (2004)
The Grid (2008)
Here Comes the Nice (2011)

Psychedelic Meadow

Jeremy Reed

Shearsman Books

First published in the United Kingdom in 2019 by
Shearsman Books
50 Westons Hill Drive
Emersons Green
BRISTOL
BS16 7DF

Shearsman Books Ltd Registered Office
30–31 St. James Place, Mangotsfield, Bristol BS16 9JB
(this address not for correspondence)

www.shearsman.com

ISBN 978-1-84861-627-1
First Edition

Cover design by Gerry McNee.

CONTENTS

For Paula Stratton and Iain Sinclair

Later, downstairs at the kitchen table,
I look round at my friends. Through light we move
Like foam. We started choosing long ago
– Clearly and capably as we were able –
Hostages from the pouring we are of.
Their faces are as bright now as fresh snow.

Thom Gunn, 'LSD, Folsom Street'

Introduction

Growing up in Jersey in the seventies, before I left to do American Studies at Essex University, wasn't easy as an anomalous poet living in a largely pedestrian, materialistic society. My escape came by way of finding part-time employment with John Berger, part of the Berger Paints family, who patented Prussian Blue, the first modern synthetic pigment. John Berger, a wealthy, reclusive aesthete and compulsive bibliophile and antiques hoarder, kept his mother mummified in the living room of his property Tivoli, and my unusual introduction to his eccentric, serendipitous lifestyle forms the basis of this sequence. If arson had torched a property of his, left as a ruin in Waterworks Valley, then the shell of the house and the adjoining fields were used by a group of friends of mine to do LSD, and to set up large speakers in the ruin through which to play psychedelic music and the seminal rock albums of the period. We called the place Psychedelic Meadow as it was regularly coloured and shaped by acid. Paula Stratton's LSD documentation of her experience of the drug became a seminal influence on my poetry. When she committed suicide in the late seventies at a squat in Chester Gate, Regent's Park a big light went out in me, and my poem 'Elegy for Paula Stratton' can be found in the collection *This Is how You Disappear*, my book of elegies for dead friends. Nobody I know has ever come more beautiful.

Prussian Blue

The Bond car
70s vermilion E-type Jag hatchback
for coastal muscle, John Berger
juicing a lick for climacteric show
the heir to Berger Paints to Prussian Blue
first modern synthetic pigment
complex colloidal dispersion
a blue that leans on black but remains blue
like watching thunder stack into a cone
he drove through, hoping to wipe age
in gene grammars, transition back
to a selective time: 12,000 tonnes
of Prussian Blue produced annually for use
in black and bluish inks. He'd done it all,
Nazi affiliation, look that blue's
Berlin blue, ferrocyanide
with legacies. Told me the commandant
in occupied Jersey bought out his shop,
mostly art nouveau vases, serious clocks
hand-painted French, money wasn't issue,
and after drank champagne sat at his desk
talking of Lewis Berger, who mixed Prussian Blue,
1760, in no better dangerous times.

The Way Down

I'd never been there, took the bunker steps
white overhead fluorescent tubes
coming on like a virtual day
I'd never see again, a bump
in time I'd tripped over,
blue paint licked on a concrete lip
like an accidental dribbled hex,
and followed his descent, the scare
worse at his back, under a house
screened out prohibitively from the road
by green confusion. Went on down
into a terminally squeezed annex
a red Nazi flag collapsed on a desk
and she was there – he'd had her mummified
his Corsican mother, her bandages
done like a toffee wrapper, the event
so awesomely irreversibly odd
it threw me out of boundaries,
her fingertips brushing the scarlet flag,
eyes redirected at her, turning round
to find the lights gone out, me on the stair.

Fruitarian + Heroin

Each his own individual way,
one banana, one Kitkat, blush pink grapes
as daily nutrition, coffee
so sticky Turkish black like impasto
spooned with Acacia honey
a meticulous fruitarian
his diet clean as marine oxygen
even his heroin
was mauve poppy. I didn't know the world
in his employment, kind of
baby I'm not here, only these words are,
sitting out my break under the skylight's
thunder-damaged polyurethane caulking
next to a pile of Virginia Woolf firsts
oxidised mustard yellow.
I'd hear him turning over rooms searching
for something located in his mind
he'd never find in flashback millennia
rumbling the silver. I was 19+
waiting to move on, already vegan,
and wore a Prussian blue lapis lazuli stone
he gave me, soaked up his reality
as paranormal, felt the house walk in
and squeeze me like a granite python.

Foggy Start

Got closer in on it than breath
Lowell's psychiatric *Life Studies, Notebook*
as diaristic cocktailed agenda,
compress the hipster world to 14 lines
a sonnet's poetry's black-box,
my mother put me on it
and Mister Prussian Blue gave me Rimbaud
like heisting a jeweller's window
into saturated psychedelics
we did hesitantly on the rooftop –
an old man tripping into the rainbow's curve,
a young man edging psychotic collapse
in a lysergic timeline that seemed years
in chromatic brilliance. Nobody knew
my teenage infatuation with madness
and my avatar's drug paraphernalia
like an occult opiated ritual.
All of his properties left to subside
into imploded stucco masonry,
bits of it missing our head, and the lot
choked with antiques sourced from the Middle-East,
China, Japan, and got like a plutocratic mogul
in a limo blasting a dust cloud out of town.

Blood Sugars

Blood glucose 184 mg/dl
    reactive hyperglycaemia the start
of needles. Valley fog so thick
    it looked like an eco-aspirin
a tufty opaque furry hangover

so tangible I'd sculpt it round my wrist
    like a vaporous octopus.
Potato Shack down bottom, strawberries
    sexualised at a red scrunch
his sunken house slung low behind a bend

like a port you wouldn't enter.
    Fog like autonomous mirage
so deep his headlights sliced through it like butter
    come back as suffocating stuff
and I got launched into *Naked Lunch* there

as a biomedical user's guide
    while he talked of money markets
and arson, how the house exploded in petrol
    and peeled the Rolls like a can
stripped by hydrochloric acid

fuckt by his attraction to Nazi leather
    and the locals labelled me for it
community with a collaborator
    but I only cared books and bottles
we drank and threw into the reservoir.

Some Books read at Psychedelic Meadow

Asa Benveniste, *Edge*, Joe Di Maggio 1976
Joseph Berke & Mary Barnes, *Two Accounts of a Journey Through Madness*, MacGibbon &Kee 1972
William Burroughs, *Naked Lunch*, Corgi, 1968
William Burroughs, *White Subway*, Aloes Books, 1973
J.G, Ballard, *The Atrocity Exhibition*, Cape,1970
J.G. Ballard, *Crash*, Cape, 1973
Edward Dorn. *Geography*, Fulcrum, 1968
David Gascoyne, *Collected Verse Translations*, OUP, 1970
Thom Gunn, *Moly*, Faber, 1971
Lee Harwood, *Landscapes*, Fulcrum, 1969
R.D. Laing, *The Divided Self*, Penguin
Christopher Middleton, *Our Flowers & Nice Bones*, Fulcrum, 1969
Stuart Montgomery, *Shabby Sunshine*, Fulcrum, 1973
John Michell, *City of Revelation*, Garnstone Press, 1972
J.H. Prynne, *Into the Day*, privately published, 1972
Iain Sinclair, *Kodak Mantra Diaries*, Albion Village Press, 1971
John Wieners, *Nerves*, Cape Goliard, 1970
John Wieners, *Behind the State Capitol*, Good Gay Poets, 1975

Dandelions

A meadow of lemon suns
or one on a doorstep
like Blake's brain
hallucinating drenched yellow
 lysergic psychosis
so even his piss created
a hologram in the street
a puddle vision in Soho
and me outside the valley house
watching their grey space-helmets
rising like Ziggy's 'Starman'
into a red-haired
Bowie sci-fi alien
time-slip fiction
like pop pollen blown from Peckham
to colonised Mars.
Never got so close to them
as sitting in forced attention
to their intense pigment
everything that makes them so
aggressively energised
driven up into the light
and got me reading Blake first time
in the middle of a field
as visionary clarity.

Floyd

Opened the meadow into psychedelics
Floyd on the exhaustive arc
of a migrant generation, Meddle
like doing sonic yoga on a breeze
floppy as lifting honey
iridescent riffy shimmers
played so loud we tore the valley open
a neighbour a mile up the road
exoplanetary terraforming Mars
on a cotil. We took over the site,
three of us in under trees
like leaves grew from our leather sleeves
in an exact involvement with geography
zippered against the skirmishing loopy fog
in the tree's sculpted armpits.
Our intermediary hormonal state –
even standing still was like riding a bike
with crotch momentum across the planet.
Floyd laid us out in the grasses,
drizzled by floaty chromatic sketches
'Pillow of Winds' under my back.
A man stood watching us up on a slope
smashed by the sound, turned round by it
like he'd got zapped by World War 3.

Strange Attractors

Glenise, stoned under his wedgy thumbprint
    at 25, a cigar
dipped in sticky sugary Sambuca
    attitude you didn't, he did
trip into another chapter

both shared the same beach-blonde hair dye
    a managed simulacrum
Boots. I'd got into her makeup
    spontaneous androgyny
co-opted into a delusional summer

like the fog was tinctured with acid
    into purple, orange, green
molecular arabesques at First Tower
    walking the beach like a space rock
a collusive community outlawed

by age inequality and local
    aspersion – the writing was very clear
spray-canned on a south facing wall
    Glenise sponged off red acrylic
as bits of chemical venom – I mean

people came like objects out of the fog
    3D spooks that couldn't take it
doing lysergic tantra and went mad
    come in out of the music to hear
time like a snake knotting its tail

Dave/Paula

Dave's blue gated aviators
did wraparound reflective sky
kept orange sunshine in the fridge
each dose a 300 mg hit
and his one sleepy eye

wobbled like gel at some reflex,
the acid man, his dope sister
came to us dispensing vision,
sit in the daisies, climb out
into the fifth-dimension…

Paula walked out of her eyes
into mine, such fluency
I felt the added chemical
of her floaty personality
mix with me like purple sunshine

They were over just for summer
slept out in the Berger ruin
got their water from a blue stream
collecting clouds in its shimmer
sat there naked in the noon sun

self-focused on patterning.
Time blew back, September yellowed
into foggy footprints, they took
a room a while, Dave's sugar cubes
fixed like a library in the fridge.

Book Striptease

Taught me their hard anatomy
spinal column brainstem
paper with a grain that bites
ink like black pepper
boards as statistical curve
jacket like a patterned dress
edge-wear as default
avoid rips along the hem
protect with a glassine condom.
Tied the needle in, shot up
bloody process heroin
halved the lesson like a grapefruit
while he collapsed into it,
got back to the colophon
as signature slot
on a limited edition,
got my knowledge bit by bit
a book's like climbing a tree
to shake down the alphabet
into readability –
no city's ever knowable
or finished, like a text's open
contained only by dimensions
8 x 5 weighed in his hands
like supporting the universe.

Dave the Dealer

A polymorphic synthesis
of scrambled personalities, but clear
drugs = money, and so thin
I'd see right through him to the light
at his centre, heart chakra
red, purple, green and blue,
a vibrational hologrammic
planet bent to his mission, deal
a vision, acid pandemic
inflecting ideologies,
but money, it was glue to him
inside his body, dug in deep
to a monetised chemistry
like gold in the hills, up there
on our makeshift summer summit
the dealer rehearsing lysergic
alchemy, me reading Thom Gunn
on making altitude
through pathways in the cells
across a field. Dave came and went
dematerialised into exhaust
a drizzled colour plume.
I treated it all as academy,
a summer process, we were moving on
inside ourselves, before October rain
came on orangey, brilliant drench
shaking a tambourine over the valley.

Paula Flies

Acid as anti-
gravity, purple hairbrush
pulled from a roomy
vermilion shoulder bag
she told me she'd started to fly
over Dannemarche reservoir
I mean into the hyper-real
adventitious orange window
giving her a levity
and there were faces in the trees
eyes that opened in the know
like they were at a festival
a 3-D Glastonbury
and she was flying as she spoke
high she said, rotatory
in a mental orbital
in which she spun
around a luminous cone
seeing through me without frontiers
flying she said to know that light
sustains the body
as a psychedelic dance
freed into pure energies

Paula

Spent afternoons reading under a tree
words verbalised as colour blocks
'reading Spenser it's always green,'
she said, 'Ballard silver
futures – when I read you
it's indigo, Kerouac black,
Tolkien's nut-brown,' she wanted gold
but only got it as pure drug
diagrammatic incunabula
come up as gold.
'A word can stay an hour in view,
it's like a planet's sidereal drift,'
she never got beyond reading
her mind and not the book:
her blue eyes, cerulean and turquoise,
reviewed hundred-thousand watt atoms
in her cells, everything foregrounded
up-close, her jet earrings black as deep space,
a market find – I mean be beautiful
like stars shine out of personality
collecting where they do in every look.

Red Dahlias

Bent round the ruin, strawberry
saturated vermilion
China red double bloom
morphologies, and deeper burgundy
swiped me like extraterrestrial stuff

in fenced time, couldn't get at them
for red guard, didn't think I'd missed
out on their place, until they broke
into awareness I was seeing them
as hyper; he told me Aztec

the valley flower – goes back to Mexico
cocoxochitl – violent red sun
and there that summer with white eyelashes
turned over by rain, faced us down
so ruby they were like neon.

A scarlet head too big for the body's
acutely anorexic stem
flower intelligence for no personnel
but some stripped private entropy,
the way it goes, like the cosmic backyard

blown out and dusted in three weeks
into amazing crisis – gone with it
the secret, like *Gone with the Wind*, he said,
too big to read, you'd walk across the Sahara
in the same time, just seeing red on red.

Great Gatsby

Cold diagnostics, took the book apart
    as issue points, 120k
like trafficking human organs, lungs, heart,
    quarter-inch fade from blue to grey
on jacket spine, a hairline fracture there,

issue points correct, showed me p.60,
    line 16, 'chatter' that got wiped
for 'echolalia' as more sexy
    like Zelda's thirteenth cocktail stripped
of brandy, before thrown into a bath

to fizzle in a twist of steam. A look,
    p.119, line 22,
'northern' for 'southern, ' he tilted the book,
    a first state jacket, it's true blue,
randomised chips, he pointed without touch

at the girl's gold irises, 'look inside
    you'll see two nudes reclining there,
a Scribner's trick, a detail made to hide
    intention' – he held back from fear
of my mishandling, reinforced his hold,

replaced the tissue protective over
    Cujat's jacket, saw the book fit
into a custom built cobalt leather
    clamshell box, inched a perfect sit
and never saw it again out its slot.

Some Music we listened to at Psychedelic Meadow

Band of Gypsies (Jimi Hendrix)
David Bowie, *Ziggy Stardust and the Spiders from Mars*
David Bowie, *Diamond Dogs*
John Cale, *Paris 1919*
Leonard Cohen, *Songs of Love and Hate*
Leonard Cohen, *New Skins for Old Ceremonies*
Curved Air, *Air Conditioning*
Cream, *Wheels of Fire*
Donovan, *Gift from a Flower to a Garden*
Fat Mattress 1 and *2*
Jimi Hendrix, *Electric Ladyland*
John Lennon/Plastic Ono Band
The Kinks, *Face to Face*
Nico, *Marble Index*
The Pretty Things, *SF Sorrow*
Dory Previn, *Mythical Kings and Iguanas*
Lou Reed, *Rock and Roll Animal*
Lou Reed, *Coney Island Baby*
Road, *Road*
Rolling Stones, *Let It Bleed*
Rolling Stones, *Sticky Fingers*
Small Faces, *Ogden Nut's Gone Flake*
Steppenwolf, *Magic Carpet Ride*
Traffic, *The Low Spark of High Heeled Boys*
The Velvet Underground & Nico
The Velvet Underground, *White Light/White Heat*
Neil Young, *On the Beach*

Sleeper in the Valley   *after Arthur Rimbaud*

A squeezed green valley, there's a stream tracks through
as silver dazzle, curves into the drop
hidden by grasses – overhead a blue
persistent hum drones from the mountaintop.

A young soldier lies with his mouth open
tangled in green confusion, head thrown back
as though he's sleeping – only look again
his posture's frozen: weeds choke up the track.

His boots are half--buried in rootsy mud,
his jaw's too slack to mistake for a smile
or imagine leaked sunshine warms his blood,

this teen deserter insects crawl inside,
one hand on his chest, it's been there a while
like the two red holes puncturing his side.

Fugitives

They grouped and formed a summer tribe,
stoned hipsters, some in leather skins
navigating a drug's pathway
in which physical boundaries
grew confused, inner and outer
losing distinction, so they lived
as substance intermediaries
migrated from the city to
an island like a green opal
puffed with iridescent haze
a sort of physical mirage –
twelve parishes – a big green field
in which to chill, fuck, come up on
induced polypharmacy
doing workable molecules
and in the process getting free
of laws written for other states
in physical geography.
Transient, nomadic, born to move
inside time for a decade
like pinching up the new into
a poem before it's written,
they brought attraction with their look
and futures culture, hung around
like a moon-landing, did it right
flying by sitting on the ground.

Interesting Weird

His pet crow Topsy, argued over cheese,
a glowering black stump of rescue
a symbiotic absorber
of how intelligence got moved
around the room – mature cheddar

chopped to a salty nugget snacked
on a pushed out red velvet couch
picked up at auction for a snip,
its brain wired with telepathy
signalling exo-dialect

to a black mob of alien hooligans?
A picky vegetarian
its primal yoga on one leg
was studied, shivery, solo,
looking at itself looking back

with no differential.
It shared a room with fifteen cats,
all veggie, intimidated
by its couch marshall effrontery
as militating psychopath.

Went for rehab into a cage,
spading at pumpkin seeds. It ruled the house
mafia-Topsy, bovver boy,
orientated to the sun
downsized inside its brain like a baked bean.

Rites of Passage

Led Zep arrived as roaming dinosaurs
Page thunder reinventing blues
as aviation futures
Stairway to Heaven on a curve
to owning the end of the world,

a kind of kamikaze Zen
inside its cone.
I watched rain coming on like liquid bees
into my time, too young to know
a nanosecond's all we get

running ourselves out of our lives…
Mostly I waited on the beach
to be alone in my surround
import vision like Chinese cars
crunched into my neuronal fit.

I didn't want to stay or go
the universe sat in my brain
compact as a second skin
and stared into a blue window
at a plane's red twinkling lights

as a generational sign.
Stood in on life close as the day
full of anxiety like fizz
watching the surf collapse, rebuild
into a hissy crunchy lisp.

KITKAT

Knuckle-cracking snap
or strip a finger clean
no fracture in the break
the red foil peeled like wallpaper
into tattered spears, silver
underside like surgery,
his one recreational hit
200 calories
of saturated booster
and got me in the habit
of this slingshot helper
shaped like a Cadillac's exhaust
as a one-a-day fetish
addictive association
of how I bled into his life
like a risk appetite
lifted his B-side not his A
as infectiously ruinous
and never got it right again
or free of his penumbra,
reminded by this scarlet pack
of damage, one to four
broken fingers, as reminders
it still goes on this legacy
I fit inside a pocket.

Purple Haze

Gypsified nomad in a red tunic
mixed race mixed reality
arrived like a transitional mirage-man
into dosed feedback distortion
guitar weaponry used to bio-hack

neural wiring – carried the times
as riff architect virtuoso
built into a generation's
nervous system, like 'Purple Haze'
house-painting a dystopia

with visionary chords
anatomising a decayed sixties
with stratospheric wah-wah commentary
pointing the way over the bridge
to a festival where a purple sun

went down on a faded meta-species,
a coshed idealism mashed
into Altamont's elemental mud.
Hendrix as journey avatar
like opening out a Western Lands river

into a muddied dope thoroughfare.
It hit our solar plexus, the bloodstream,
Electric Ladyland mixed up in us
as generational soundtrack, his noise
building a cone to flatten a mountain.

Some esoteric names for LSD used by Dave and Paula

Orange Sunshine

Lazy Sunshine Dust

Purple Haze

Lucy in the Sky with Diamonds

Alice

Windowpane

Sunshine Superman

Uncle Sid

Strawberry Glow

Eight Miles High

Glow

Bardo Thodo

UFO dots

White Rabbit

These names for acid, drawn from psychedelic rock references or the inspired chemical vision sometimes mentally documenting a mini-death/rebirth experienced in the user, were also a selling point in that the specific name implied the possible experience to be encountered in the drug's psychoactive pathways. Dave as simultaneous user and dealer found it hard to dissolve the boundaries between either.

Coming Down Again

The DROP's like crashing out of one decade
into another, all the way
100,000 ft
in inner space, we played it too
in gradations of red and green and blue
track 3 on *Goat's Head Soup*
like parachuting down on a snowflake
in winter to arrive summer
with no delay at all.
You see a diagram sharpening your mind
like aliens exist, come through
on Martian desert radio
in local space. You don't know one decade
sorted from another when you've no past
but living in it, read *Lud Heat*
as signal of seventies geography,
place as extension of body
like fitting an exhaust. Came back to it,
his fire-blackened front-door, blistered,
torched, big creamy elderflowers
fisting attention as musty saucers,
and hung back, afraid kicking it open
I'd meet an explosive cone of red flame
fanning its zigzag surges round my feet.

Drink

Green-walled Perrier-jouet
he'd give us: its amazing solar stream
carbonated bubble rush
of gold fizz in a paper cup
us collapsed in grasses –
'what would you do on your last day?'
she asked me, 'compress it all down
into crunched bits, a start an end
your whole life on a biscuit?'
Paula looked up into the sun
desegregated brain networks
working out where she was in time
proportionate to space,
and final endings, work it out
like a disappearing airstrip
a truncated red carpet
disappearing down a stairwell
into a disused tunnel.
'I'd want to see the friends who mean
intimate to me, take me down
to where my mother waits, still blonde in death,
behind a screen. I'd leave a thought
as molecular snapshot.'
We drank two bottles, heard his bashed Daimler
approach the valley like an armoured car
headlights full on despite the blinding sun.

In the Middle

Read Ballard for a brain refit,
neural re-wiring, a total
rehab, the only fiction spiked
with rokit science, techie know,
biomedical metaphor,
sci-fi lingo
I got off on, sniffed its exhaust
as legal high, took up its build
as transmissible to poetry,
sold on the Panther 1972
Atrocity Exhibition pbk
as filmic psychopathological menu –
transplant brains, Marilyn Monroe's yantra,
a white chromed-up Pontiac full of cum
and iconic mastectomies on video.
Changed everything in my makeup
like going orbital, preferred
neural architecture and nano-meds,
pharma giants, hot cellulose
to landscape, switched my own bacteria
to off-world, like getting mind-fuckt,
and look at me now, all my unread books
grown over by wild grasses in our summer meadow.

Cultdom

All those under-inked mimeos
on confetti-coloured over-
absorbent paper
as indie poetry – you miss a phrase
and rewrite it for yourself
as better, like skipping one reality
to make another, do it everyday
as iridescent fiction, saw them out
Joe DiMaggio, Sixpack, Ant's Forefoot
as motivated attractors
a sort of subversive academy
as thing. Summer stretched slowly like yoga
in trancy mirage – I could see my thoughts
like snapshots taking shape in dazzled glow
the distances I walked into
like a film studio.
Got them in jiffies, Albion Village Press
with Sinclair notes, made it into the game
as undercover, someone who didn't exist
to writing, working on a language soup
like mixing alphabetic impasto
to a blue pigment bluer than the sky.

I was writing into and for myself, saturated in the compressed imagery employed by the likes of Rimbaud and Hart Crane, and grew fixated on Crane's boozed-up, dissipated photos, as a poet who'd lived so totally for his art to the exclusion of all material interests I took him for a psychic avatar. Crane's notorious pursuit of sailors, together with his jobless, often itinerant life, and the dynamic fuelling his all or nothing approach to what he wrote set him apart in my mind from anyone else I'd read. The way he'd committed suicide in 1932 at the age of thirty-one by jumping off the stern of the SS Orizaba at exactly noon, into the Caribbean, stuck with me as the paradigm for the way some totally committed poets lived and died. I sent a batch of my unreadable dense youthful poems to George Barker, a poet I greatly admired, who replied that I'd 'been bitten in the calf by the Muse,' and suggested I go visit him, so that together we could 'throw salt over the devil's tail.' Through George passing my work on to Asa Benveniste, the cult publisher who issued books from his Trigram Press, Asa shocked me by flying to Jersey to visit me on a foggy summer day with the request he publish a book of mine. Asa's support, generosity, and genuine love of my work helped me out of some bad, self-harming places, and it was on his insistence I left Jersey to go study at the University of Essex. Dressed all in black, he became the man in black for me, a thin chain-smoking mentor, who was immersed in kabala and image-based language as the occult resources of poetry. Asa's letters to me encouraging my start outs in poetry, and his continuously gifting me with books he thought I should read as seminal to my own development gave me enough self-belief to leave my inhibitively restricted island birthplace and go study before taking up with life in London.

Asa

This man, he came to me wanting a book,
so thin he looked like a rope trick,
piano black shirt, black skinny jeans,
alchemical Jewish magus
soft-spoken American-flavoured baritone
inflected with Camel smoke, so cool
he seemed to epitomise postmodern
and me so insularly emergent
I needed a sign to get out, go where
my poems projected – he said
'a Trigram book, maybe 30 poems,
you know that's 300 in your language
that crunches a Boeing to a tin can.'
We walked a mile in iridescent haze
talking abstract – planes lowering overhead
in smoky plumes – we stopped to drink some wine
talking of long-haul sunshine, yellow dust,
the journey into photosynthesis.
A book? – it seemed the start of an identity,
concretised object into which I'd fit
myself as scrambled rehearsed alphabet.
Asa said, 'poetry won't change your life,
it's what Li Po called permanent autumn,
just think chrysanthemum, a yellow fade
that's slow – you go with it all the way down,
you get one reader, you've got company.'

Let Me Take you Down

Like Andy's yellow banana
peelable off the VU sleeve
a parabolic curve
the bend – torque on a Mercedes
clean as frictional lube
his way to Strawberry Fields
down four Victorian flights
top to bottom, neural
circuitry slipped out of time
like a plane takes a curved path
flying from London to New York
a straight line's too long
the slip's via Greenland
like parts of a song
no line consecutive to another
all those lyric air-miles
compressed into three minutes
of trancing it downstairs
'let me take you down'
a decade a second
into continuum
go that way a yellow bulb
burns at the end
like a greenish pear
and the drop's where the future
tips a strawberry glow.

Fuckt

You take a Darwin first as ordinary
Baudelaire's *Les Fleurs du mal* as slumming it
the inscription a lurid trope
and it comes back to gritty ontology
no connection between person and thing,
just alienation wanting more
psychic filler, a pot, a ring,
more nothing
like looking for a dead friend on the tube
a minute or ten years too late.
Accumulate – he'd go for that
endorsement – loot
the world into his bowels, gold shit
as plutocratic hedge-funding,
argue it he'd throw a Ming at the wall
and piss on debris. All of it
as petulant malicious acrimony.
Sometimes I'd catch the sun through the window
like holding an intangible grapefruit
composed of light. He'd smash rather than sell
or give: 'everything's the same as nothing,'
go for illusion and you've got the real.

Psychedelic Meadow

Take five – you've a community
a generation excerpted from law
merging the dubious binaries
of drugs and poetry,
blow a dandelion's glittery halo

it's a cosmic event,
like reading Tarot in a field
of scattered poppies, yellow, blue and red
as extraterrestrial visitors
there for a day, singular to our lives

me seeing you seeing me
through the flower as intermediary
like we're each sitting one side of the sun
as a red transparency.
Our summer meadow seemed a planetary

discovery, self-expansive –
you walk a metre cross a mile
like inflating a stone to an asteroid,
geography remade by the eye
into holographic patterning.

Purple allium in a corner
like fisty tennis balls, just there a week
and so inclusive they seemed messengers
 in iridescent fiction – journeyers
touched in for info before moving on.

Carrefour Selous

Left of Hamptonne's rumbled barns,
Becquet Vincent, he'd dumped the DB2
in trees, a flaky, oxidised, sage green
Aston Martin, rejected like rocket parts,
gunned over with a swastika,
oodles of grey leather upholstery
prototypical design ergonomics
abandoned as luxurious decay
a shock vehicle left like a crashed plane.
A pre-Bond speed bomb capriciously rejected,
we hung around it, what to do
with creativity, couldn't convert
it into practicable reality,
all those wavelengths of psychic ideograms
like telepathic postings, didn't know
a place for them, not in community
this isotopic mixed pursuit
I knew as poetry and couldn't sell
what seemed like poking a finger through thought
as weightless molecules, waited my time
as part of his madly deregulated family.

Alchemy

You start with nothing
and it's gold
like the treasure voyages of Zheng He
or urbanisation of exos
the US flag territorialising Mars
its limp, red, white and blue PR
signposting highways to the stars
as space economy. Asa told us
read Robert Fludd
Hermes Trismegistus – gold in their veins
and closer in Rimbaud, Leonard Cohen
beating on a gold pentagram
to lead armed gangs into Jerusalem.
The arms economy, it's a numerical haiku
he told us, dragging on a joint
figures light as a purple opium poppy
in a breezeless trance. He shifted a ring
as gold confirmation, and sun filtered
into our eyes as a transmissible galaxy
get there at light speed, like it found us out.

Neural

Ballardian build
never bothered with another
futures avatar, just *Crash*
as automotive ergonomics
ripped literature like paint-stripping a car
into a virtual figure
an urban realisable techspeak
like the moon's managed biosphere
was closer than a golf ball
found smacked into the garden.
Absorbed his post-apocalyptic
 trashed eco-collapse
reading it all like tomorrow
lived in my brain as a diamond
coded with isometric rooms
in which mixed reality happened.
Started it soonest I found
luridly covered time-slip paperbacks
branding sci-fi dystopia
as psychedelic domain,
copied out every line appealed
into a collaged diagram
learning my way book by book
into Zen as torched-up rocket fuel.

Looking for a new window on poetry to invite a language from tomorrow, I found it in the projective, futuristic short stories and novels of J.G. Ballard, whose biomedical, neuro-scientific, smart-tech terminology was the one most instantly appealed to my needs to inject a whole new range of near futures experience into poetry. I see Ballard as the great poet of the mid to late 20th-century, his compressed dystopian imagery outdistancing anything British poetry offered in its slow retro-crawl backwards on blown out tyres. Ballard's exhaust plume was for me the one to follow, like one Boeing taking off into another's hot vaporised fuel. I liked too the fact that Ballard really didn't have any contemporaries, but lived on the edges of inclusion in literature as a rogue bandit, more likely to be reading data issued by NASA scientists than the pedestrian footprint of mainstream fiction. There wasn't and still isn't anyone near to Ballard in overtaking language as apocalyptic travelogue. He got into my system from the start like a serious dependency – a Ballardian substance to which I'm still habituated. His introduction to my book of poetry West End Survival Kit, done at his request, after he'd been an enthused reader of my poetry for decades was for me an endorsement like silver dazzle paint on my often kicked reputation for going his way.

Zero divided by Zero

At Saville House, cerulean ceilings
or creamy cyan, his tropical aviary
of stuffed birds decayed under glass,
Victorian taxidermy
looked like a bird junta installation
a ravaged guerrilla war. He shot up
behind a Chinese screen, came on again
normalised, Paula fingering a rip
got high left leg in revamped jeans,
a jet necklace he'd given at her throat
like matt lapidary voodoo,
something he said worn for mourning, a black
like achromatic hair, the house peeling
its topcoat flakily. His small snapshot
of a car getaway from stationary –
t seconds = txt metres,
the car goes faster in the second half second
from 10 to 11, lost on us, and he
distractively preoccupied with books
and what was circulating in his veins
as heavy industry, and we had toys,
a house stuffed to its summit with antiques
like climbing a glass mountain to the sky.

Losing It Young

Limited timeline written in our veins,
how can you cross a thousand years
and make it back to a meadow
with the same physiology,
those times we lived through haven't arrived yet,
a generation gone,
Paula's suicide, David's OD,
I'm waiting for their reinsertion
in my continuous reality
to sit there in the dandelions
as though what happened in between
was an illusory time-loop,
a means of never letting go a decade
in which we saw behind our eyes
4D availability, the space
where aliens rehabilitate to Earth
by bio-hacking. We sat in on it
in such an orange purple strawberry glow
it seemed our own unsustainable brilliance,
like all we ever had in arriving
at our domain, dusty with grass seeds, broke,
richer in vision for owning nothing.

Visitors from the Future

Time's like a sandwich, can't remake
ingredients – humus, falafel, red shredded
cabbage, bite into 1970s
you get a futures flavour from a past
declassified, pinch up our days
like tribal immigrants from the exosphere

who left no trace, just the indifferent stand
of nature crashing, maybe trees still there
choked up by ivy's viral pandemic
and me writing this into empty space
in a Starbucks window watching rain scatter
in spiral ziggurats over the street.

There's something in the distortion of light
remains, a time-frame, a digitised code,
some bit imported and so quantum-quick
I sense it sometimes, and if it exists
it's in the wishing the story carries
some reclamation, just a little hit

of recognition to transcend regret.
Maybe we lost it before it happened
as figures spaced in trees – I see us still
winning a vision, losing it again,
but so informed we thought we had it all
in brilliant moments brighter than the light.

Glenise

Incredulously mind-
fucked, boozed for words
rummaging in a biscuit tin
for sweet reward, a fat cigar
dipped in sloe-gin
sucked to an orange glow
like an exhaust core
and fuming at his monomaniacal
idiosyncratic demands
go find something lost 30 years
and lose it in the process
all over again,
like backpacking across China
searching for a button.
She never stood a chance
so mentally disadvantaged
kicking at his errands
like she'd balled his crotch
her aggro turned in
as volatile retainer
to self-harm – look that cut
it's like a Bakewell tart
sliced to Leonard Cohen's
terminal *Songs of Love and Hate*
like she always crossed the river
too early or too late.

One Big Jewel

Take a diamond big as the sun
it's a lysergic molecule
lending Paula micro-gravity
never knew it she sat in a tree
all day, shaken down by rain
as fractal lozenges
a Persian rug irised in each drop
as iridescent ruby-blue arabesques
she told me, hallucinated,
coming dreamy out of the shower
into mixed reality.
There's one big jewel that's poetry
orbits a sound cone in my brain
told that as affirmation
of vision, words as they dance in patterns
I didn't make happen
in standing up right
as six pips on a fallen dice.
A day in the trees you learn all
about what's in you and out
and the dissolve where it all happens
like finally being inside the light.

Dope Sister

Sharing her black woollen greatcoat
our two skinny shoulders dissolving
body-temperature boundaries,
vintage, high collar
Portobello snip
thrown as a wrap against puffed fog
together – she had to go
telling me to split geography
like pitting an avocado
get to the capital where poetry
lives in the centre of the world
right under Piccadilly – where was that
until I found it? – dark came on
building opposition against the sun
right on our shoulders deliquescent mist –
the poet at the centre of his shape,
she said, inverting ordinary reality,
and promised I'd get over, Strawberry Hill,
walkable to where Virginia Woolf lipped
the current's squishy froth, nostrils open
to swirling Thames – the river dived in there
choking her lungs, hallucinated surge,
and my first London stay in an attic
wallpapered outside by orange splashy chestnut leaves.

Strawberry

Heart-shaped demonstrative red
like a San Paulo pout
it scrambles the senses like pepper
thrown in front of a cat,
a sensual push-out of its seams
to popped juicy vivacity –
its unsunned conical tip
an intimate privacy
like temper shimmering off
into fried atmosphere,
a strawberry gene don't come redder
than overhyped vermilion
as red insanity
or a Ferrari skin.
June, they're on my palate
I'm picky with their texture
like existential flavour,
biting into life as variable
I'd make singular
like that one face in the crowd
sorts from the millions
as individually special,
its oddly familiar focus
like this elusive taste I go back to
because I can't remember.

1970s Books

Their physicals face me face out
as occupied space in my life
mostly Barry Hall jackets or Asa's
subversively chewy
  orange and yellow lipsticks licks

psychedelic, on the moment,
titles in punky graffiti
or stylised fonts like a Sudoku box
keeps lettering on the line.
There's a pioneering UK trio

Cape Goliard, Trigram, Fulcrum,
hosting American-flavoured
poetry as streetish lingo.
Menuish, freed-up, gossipy,
right in the shape like detail

in jeans or aqua car gloss.
There's *Big Green Day* or Jim Dine's
Welcome Home Love Birds, or Lee's
The White Room (surname Harwood)
or Maximus as psychogeography

Ed Dorn's *Gunslinger* 1& 2
as sharpshooter tactics in Joanna,
they're like a mortuary slab
in my life, a juiced currency
printed on high end paper

a 1970s dip-in block
still feeding me tactile aesthetic
and a love of the book as atlas
spatializing how words dance
on toe-points into blue eyes.

China Quarry Farm

Christiane's and psychotropics
if you do magic mushrooms –
Liberty Cap troops of psilocybin
as indigenous undercover aliens –
and you'll find her D-cup conical topless
in summer, splashed by chocolate moons
on an oval lawn, the house back
18th-century quarried granite
Starbucks green paint like their logo
licked onto flaky frames.
St Lawrence – a croissant-shaped parish
oaks marking out its borders
dense as thunder clouds, nail polish glossy.
Visit when I need magic as resource
psychic care like a new jumper
put on to help me through
breaking another window in my nerves
smashing it like a skyscraper's
disintegration. Christiane rights me
into magnetic symmetry adjust
or something like it standing under trees
the way we do green healing in that space
with all those transcendent healing energies.

You Think I Care

Writing a poem a day
like popping a time-slip pill
a verbal hallucinogenic
it's easy as cracking a chocolate
digestive, or a car seller's stat
for a 0.65 mph grunt
in 3 seconds, that easy
like ball-chains on the zippers
of a biker's leather jacket dragged to open
a heart-side pocket–
do it facilitating pathways
across destabilised frontiers
like I'm in a personal time zone
floating autonomously
over borders where morning glories
are bluer than bluest sky
a toned-up exuberant turquoise
ain't on no colour chart.
Don't get nothing but contempt
for doing what I do
so stay with it, no other way
of owning to reality
or calling this mad pursuit art.

I was with Asa one afternoon at 22 Leverton Street, his open-plan conversion back of Kentish Town station, his silver wool and silk crewneck remarking on his zero size, on my way back to Jersey. He said to me, one hand slipped into a jeans pocket, 'there's no one I want to publish, Prynne's like a barrister, Zukofsky petulantly argues against my edition, I can't find the language I'm looking for as poetry. There's no gold.' He was drinking Cutty Sark, his choice of whisky, and I could see his expectations for poetry were right down low. He was always reading alchemy, a bit like his black on black slingshots of Turkish coffee, and had found a passage from Walter Raleigh, that I remembered his reading out loud and later re-found to give you. 'When they are anointed all over, certain servants of the emperor, having prepared gold made into fine powder, blow it through hollow canes upon their naked bodies, until they be all shining from the foot to the head.' I think Asa saw the internal residents of a poem as like that, gold imported into language won from lexical turmoil. He'd take the word as ultimate unit, polarised black opacity, cabalistic digit concealed in peanut butter, world code-breaker, its elusive serial generated circadian rhythm, it was math crunched into metaphor. Tarot, the Zohar, *I Ching*, he looked for the accident in them like a grass seed shipped to Alpha Centauri. Every line he wrote was a shine on it, an approximate resonance; an attempt to make the occult domestic. It wore him thin, but language was our talk and effort, the poem's calories burnt on the line. He'd turned down John Ashbery's *Three Poems*; then discovered they were partially what he was looking for in the search. We went out later to Compendium where Asa marvelled at Christopher Dewdney's neuro-scientific diction and bought us each copies of *Fovea Centralis* and *A Palaeozoic Geology of London Ontario*. They're as close to me this day, as then.

Diet Candy

My brain-mapping's like Area 51
declassified off-world crashed UFO site
framing a sky pink as Turkish Delight
sliced by an Airbus' shimmering fins,
a wonky abstract skyline diagram
my capital affairs. I threw you out

as saturation, copy of my style
requiring editing – the back of you
my restart, back to blue, in Africa
they decommission AK-47s
Congo rifles recycled to optimal steel,
the conversion shocks, tribal cannibals

4 candy, semi-precious stones like sweets
in gorgeous colours. What's this got to do
with luxurious lilacs drenched in scent
doing their seasonal update – me and you
lacked gold resources: lilacs stumping up
like some elongated crazy dessert

glazed violet. What I remember hurts,
the memory cells touch-sensitive today
with bruises like your heels walked over me
at Steele's Village, windy white chestnut flowers,
transitioning through Chalk Farm, cherry clouds
compacted into scoops over the canal.

Somebody's barbecuing buffalo
in fatty smoke drags. It's veggie war
on my side, vegan-clean meat-free protein
against popping sine was urban flesh-snatchers,
takes me back to our V-diet – that green
it lived in us like clear spatialised Zen,

and stays a window into energies,
the ones I value for their valency.
What we've got marked out as a sort of share
meshes residual good with things that crashed
and now lilacs regroup with clustered tusks
and stay a moment steady on the air.

B.S.

Johnson
Kentish Town truculent
maverick elephant
his solo fiction surgery
scrambling linear
into *I Ching*
a bottle of Famous Grouse
his signposting instructor
Aren't You Aren't You Aren't You
Far Too Young to Be Writing Your Memoirs
it's timing good as Sinatra's
spacing a phrase
it's the poet in him that rocks
my metabolic juices
Poems and *Poems Two*
tight as a panic attack
and hands on like scooping shingle
on a Thames beach for gold.
It's the imaginary slices
into my visual frames
rude attitude infecting
everything he did as loner
irascible liver fatty
loser, giving words a helium lift,
slashing his wrists in the bath
like Beaujolais – the edit
a half bottle of brandy left
for whoever found him dead.

Get Back

Sometimes the light at the table, you're it,
like a decade sat there, this orange sun
like internal resident of a gland
reinvents futures deposit,
you sit one knee up, back against the wall,
holding your hair behind your neck
in twisted spills, root-dyed tumbles, red, gold,
invasive black – it's ethnobotany
the psychoactives in your smoke
that smell like grilled weather. There's Dave's fat roll
of twenties done up in a rubber band,
time stuck like a drinking straw in a glass
left fizzing. Transition back to real time
and endgame predictions, a big red sun
like neon fission, migrant hordes
of no-people standing in blinding rain,
psychopathic oligarchs on the run
in gated jeeps. The light comes up again
including you, and it's a brilliant cone,
chrysanthemum yellow, like we're re-made
as insert in some reversed-time snapshot
in which our immediate energies glow.

Unlimited Inspiration

Hangs on biographical pegs
the idea of Paula scrunched into words
the wreckage of her past in me
and flippant iridescent rain today
or any vacant unctuous longueur
in which she opens into consciousness
like a red nipple on a thought,
her suicide part of fascination
I can't unstructure, only elevate
the way she dropped off the planet
at 26. A fist of pills,
white benzos as vertiginous way down,
it becomes something else over the years
an understanding of commitment to
a shared vision we'd rather lose
than modify. Sometimes I think she's back
or I'll get a predictive text
from one million light-years away
some place she'll tell me gives a better chance
to our type; and she died at Chester Gate,
ten pounds in her red bag, like all she had,
and every cell in her a visionary diamond.

If decades were stored in cryonic pods like people, we'd be able to retrieve blocks of time and review the past. A 1970s movie lasting 87,600 hours would be viewable in a decade of real time, if you wanted the whole thing. Where are the seventies, as the subject of this poem, back of you, or upfront, as still having not yet arrived? Is my poem an imagined remake in the catalogue of missing time, or is it engineered by what's around me now, visually present in the Starbucks where I'm writing? I'm always surprised in terms of organ trafficking that nobody attempts to hijack specific generational genes, like a sixties or seventies gene for the data it stores and traces of the cultural revolution of those times coded into synapses.

Was the sunshine at Millbrook Vale Chalet, the site of our psychedelic meadow less light polluted, so a brighter orange? Summer's immediate to every generation, but back then it seemed to carry optimal focus as a workable energy in which to bring about accelerated changes, not only creatively, but ideologically. Maybe our summer lasted what seemed a decade a month because we lived in altered time, not systemised time, so that you could feel the elasticated moment expand by delivering its contents, rather than just happening as a continuously transitional empty unit. If you can read what the moment imports you're on the way to poetry, like Rimbaud's association of the vowels with individual colours.

I'm writing this on the curve of another century. I'm not looking back I'm futures forward; whatever I ship from the past is conditioned by the present into a new reality. I'm maybe sitting out in Leicester Square sighting the trancy drift of anonymous pedestrians, while I'm engaged also in recreating biography, and the two sit comfortably. So much of what happened at Psychedelic Meadow – the ruined chalet was torched in 1968, leaving an abandoned house, that only now am I starting to remember what I'd thought had gone missing. John Berger had lost a fortune in books and antique furniture to arsonists and the residual ash got into our skin. I remember finding little grey snowflakes of it in my boots and smudges on my jeans. The sunlight when it filtered through dense trees arrived after eight minutes travel time from the sun. The valley around was empty and we replaced people with the loud reverberation of rock music riffing heavy guitar figures into unoccupied space. The crash of 'Purple Haze' starting unannounced through valley fog seemed to me to carry a purple footprint. I thought all life was that, living on the edges of reality to better concentrate on imaginative input. It worked for me; I'm still doing what I did back then, sit in on the present a hundred years before it arrives.

Temazepam

Matt white 10 mg circular moons
a seventies push-down for insomnia
fuzzy anti-anxiety warheads
a bendy psychoactive attractor,
favourite suicide sweet, bankable pills
for end-things, kept a topped-up armoury,

prescription or sourced like a take-away
from dealers: it was always her resource,
obsessively maintained security,
her investment stock, like a silo full
of stashed missiles, she never gave away
a single one, or used, just saved the lot

as dependable killers sealed in foils
like bodies in cryonic pods, and lived
with their potential – 300 maybe
in labelled boxes – I can see them still
the one time I found her sat on the floor
counting her total, a black polished nail

stabbing each film-coated pill one by one
as available quotient. Took trust
to do it finally, the drug's pathways
mapping a closure and her breathing stopped
behind the booze-accelerated shape
building inside her as the way it ends.

Wrong and Right

A spoon bevelled in Jersey marmalade,
whiskey-doused blood orange, red pulpy core
for start-up, technicolour mood
tinting the day, a pink grapefruit
like a wobbly Saturn moon, local light
having space vanish, so we reached a place
without arriving – did I see it right
future of futurology,
me reading out a poem on my breath
kinetically – the red shreds on your toast
looking like logs in a translucent glaze,
the label handwritten as Meadow Farm,
how long does it take for a poem to arrive
2053 soonest
you said, as imported immediacy.
We made convergent moments, look at time
it's like a silver nitrate wave patterned
with serial codes, you'd worked that out
from direct light. Breakfast in full July
we'd never see again in quite that way
tracking yellow diamonds between the leaves.

You start seeing dark objects if you're addicted to benzos, and that's a right lesson for poetry, and why I value my blocks of drug dependency. There's so much stuff inclusive in a sort of neural exosphere that you miss if you're not altered. I read the B's, Ballard, Burroughs, Brautigan to encounter what I live in as reality rather than fiction. If I read mainstream fiction I invariably contact too big a dose of pedestrian routine. At Psychedelic Meadow it was like we were testing frontiers right on the bleed of inner and outer space. Is what I'm looking at me, or has it separate identity? What we didn't want or care about is material entanglement, careerism as a substitute for uncompromised individuality – I'd rather be me than a social status, or identified by what I own. We were students of our own inner voyaging, I've been there all of my life, at speed, like I'm overtaking myself rather than the highway, in the way Jimi Hendrix is more playing his neurology than a guitar. 'Purple Haze' is brain rather than chord noise.

The deeper we advanced into Waterworks Valley, the denser the wooded trees. You didn't answer to anyone, because it was the green zone, maybe a farm where no one showed, the three dark green reservoirs, and John Berger's ruin where we congregated, a granite chalet, as one of his four properties used as storage for his serendipitous attachment to books and antiques. We hung out there, and being essentially a lawless bohemian, drugs, progressive fashion and rock as aspects of youth culture didn't much bother him. He'd thrown sex parties in the chalet, had the occupying German commandant and his spin-doctors there. We were simply an exciting phenomenon pushing youth forward into a future we hadn't yet reached. The sexual weird rumoured to surround him in his relations with his mother wasn't a problem with us. His admissions to me of incest were simply like auto parts to be built into a poem. I was listening a lot to Lou Reed's *Berlin* and *Sally Can't Dance* as noirish rock, narratives of drag queens, domestic violence, attempted suicide, urban sleaze, late night dystopias, so was partly acclimatised to whatever came up in what he told me. Psychedelic Meadow was the first of my subversive academies. Others were to follow in London, but this was the initial matrix that taught me never to fit in. I mean if you're polarised to literature and its social media, you can't see how ridiculously small you look inhabiting a safe space. If you stay outside you're disinhibited and free to write without being a writer. I design images; it's what I do. I express them through poetry and that's cool. What does that make me?

The oxidised gates, ivied over that provided access to the ruined house were to me the portal to a space where I could liberate imagination into its unstoppable potentialities, win or lose. I'd sit on a stone, head full of internalised white noise, and get off on my friends as alien input. It was like snapshotting mental images as they came on through. I never knew if the experience was language, or if the visual activated words. Paula believed poets have an extra chromosome, a gene specific to making it happen through brain processes that you can't access if you don't have it. Her link was somewhere paranormal that equally I couldn't reach. All I knew was that most of what influenced me came from imagined growth of the domestic as subject into a poetry as modern as sunshine arriving. I hadn't got it yet, but the formula was there for later use.

John Berger taught me books as physical aesthetic, and how they are monetised dependent on their state. I'd already assembled a library with my mother's help before I got sucked into the mad architecture of his book stacks, and the thrill of what I might find in those pillars. He obsessively sorted through each of his four properties on a daily basis, as the incalculable index of possessions he could never catalogue or properly categorise, or do anything with but add to and hoard. It was an objects field he was unable to downsize, a chaos in which he was immersed continually. And me, I carved him into poetry, used every characteristic of his weirdness to write. I'd begun the process of stealing personalities and reconstructing them like Battenberg cake. You pick at the marzipan to get at the jam grid, like a pink chessboard. He, Glenise, Paula, Dave, me, all the rest got written up in the mix and in the process became real fictions. Psychedelic Meadow is still there, conscripted now into what is Railton Hall, built on the site of the abandoned Millbrook Vale Chalet. It's a gated, tree-screened fortress with smoked-out jeeps in the drive and wraparound cameras. Our history's written out by the stacking up of the present into new lives, new times. We're not there, but in the photos we are, and it feels like a hole opened in time. What if the photos lied, how we would ever get back to the place as our time that I'm writing up in my time.

Asa used to say a good poem is a visitor from tomorrow – you don't travel with it and it comes back in its own time after disappearing off the system. It's why most mainstream poems are time-limited to the immediate present and can't manage time-slips to get out and get back different from when they were written.

Listening to the Velvet Underground in Woods

Green sunshine diffused like a green lemon
through frisky lozenges, and seemed a first
each time that garage punk came up
like a turbo-car's tuned exhaust –
a Ferrari locked into a bedroom
a drone like Chinese girl gang martial arts
done on a wooden floor, the vocal cold
as a cryonic pod, the tone
like pushing drugs on a mean hub,
and that ostrich guitar, a choppy lope
played flat like wet feet on a diving board.
We'd got it import for the chosen ones,
loud arty aggro like work on the docks
done in a studio. It levelled us
the cone of noise like take-off interspersed
with chamber moments, the band as light bulb
inside a foggy halo, moving back
into the quiet corners of a song.
We'd set up system, got the thunder loud
edge of green density, a corridor
of propulsive noise carried us up on
into the destination of the track
leaving a black exhaust plume from the roar.

I Fought the Law and the Law Won

Came to us with his Bobby Fuller tag
blue suede Desert boots grassed over
as damp toe points, a meadow scuff
on urban wear, a loser down
in everything he'd lost – you know
he'd made a boy in public
got on camera, came to Psych Meadow
with his credentials, who I am
is right as any dandelion
in its hyper-yellow identity,
his job gone – what's the best way moving out
one change into another, one
step outside time into the river,
kept coming back to our community,
pushing out frontiers, feeling grips
on personal geography, got whacked on wine
as somewhere else to go, didn't get right
for weeks, made the valley into safe space,
a steadying like standing under trees,
hearing the light, then disappeared for good.

Hydrangeas

Sapphire mopheads, a two-bit violet-pink
hybrid extravaganza, morphed colours
bled into sensational two-tone
or three, we got fixed on the clump
like an alien find, a mini-moon
too large for emotion to get around
in heady or thick weather, off the road
like a blue Mars, a damp installation
of excerpted Asian cultivars
chromosome number $2n=26$,
though you don't see it, and unstoppably
expensively gorgeous in tone
as piled on pigment, stacked design
as bluest blue. We'd go to them
looking for something in ourselves, a way
of sighting new realities,
jump one day of the week for another,
see if it comes back twice the same.
A robust cluster fuming to burn-out,
they seemed a marker, pointer on the road
as blues to almost getting anywhere.

You're (We're) Gonna Die

Edge-of-destruction feel in floaty fog
puffy as white hydrangeas.
At 20, death's a close abstract,
its password Sylvia Plath –
never thought it would come up soon
all her vitamins thrown out
of circulation.
Maths in the breathable glitter
of valley mist as fuzzy puffs,
tequila in a paper cup
and she said, 'maybe it's already happened,
my death, and I need to catch up
with the event horizon
meet who I am without a body.'
Sweet coned purple buddleia tusks
poked through vaporized figures
as haiku combinations.
I felt it creep through my blood,
one of us dead, unknowable
in that window, and it was her
as the one sucked forward so fast
she left nothing but her suede knee boots behind.

Our favourite dessert

Ingredients

Poire au Cassis   (Poached pears in red wine and cassis)

6 tablespoons redcurrant jelly

1 tablespoon port or sweet sherry

pinch powdered cloves and cinnamon

1 tablespoon orange juice

2 tablespoons brown sugar

1 dessert spoon cornflower

8 cloves

Method

Core pears from the base, place in a buttered ovenproof dish. Dissolve the redcurrant jelly, powdered cloves, cinnamon, brown sugar in the port or sherry and orange juice, making liquid up to half a pint with water, boil to form syrup. Pour over pears, bake in moderate oven for 12--15 minutes, strain off syrup. Mix with blended cornflower, bring to the boil; cook until transparent. Serve cold.

The Jersey Cook Book of St Helier by Joan Woodhall

Where We Were and Where We Are Now

Normal people don't need to write, their dialect is social exchange and not solitary focus on remaking a scientifically acceptable reality into so many alternative realities in the multiverse. If Valium hadn't already fucked up my neural wiring, then collusive strangers coming on to me in my teens, store thieves, older men wanting sex with me, weirdos with ambivalent motives, and a total absorption into pop/rock had all prepared me for my unlikely meeting with John Berger, guru of weird obsessions. My vulnerability, if it opened me to underworld influences, also mapped compensatory pathways into poetry as the mainline activity of the reality I personalised as my own creative resource. I'm still surprised that nobody else in poetry mines the same territory, I've always been looking out for some sort of clone, but my extreme originality of subject matter isn't easily copyable. Not that I care, I keep to my own.

When John Berger told me about his sexual relations with his mother, who was then mummified, I wasn't shocked. I just thought of it as something I'd metabolise for writing. It wasn't any stranger than a Velvet Underground song, and my head was and still is full of Lou Reed. That monotonal drawl casually narrating the underside of character has always been my marker as to how to build poetry out of the marginalised into epic mythmaking. I'm not interested in the socially acceptable who can't individuate into altered realities. That's why I'm an edge-walker – I prefer the bottom of the glass to the top.

And why do certain images or geographies stick like synaptic wraparounds occupying accessible space in the mind? Why can I at any selective moment find Paula rummaging in her roomy maroon bag on the concourse at Piccadilly Circus underground, searching for cash to buy a wrap of street heroin. Even the ozone pollutant whiff of the station comes back, and the sleazy fluorescents, and the sunglassed pull of the skinny dealer, his gated identity and angular cheekbones compounding mystique to his fidgety paranoia. For some reason I want to be absorbed into his identity as an extension of my own. When Paula buys she disappears to the Ladies and comes back twenty minutes later re-regulated by the drug. By that time I've been made over by hundreds of eyes streaming off the escalator in transition to the exits.

Or we're down in the valley, killing time by drugging it into our slowed-down visual frames, like we've arrested biology to work with and not against us. I'm able to sit in the day like a green window and the poppy I'm looking at has 40,000 petals, each one a different squirt of yellow. You ever seen 40,000 petals and relocated back to yourself?

There's certain people who chemically dye you and who you can never get out of your system. John Berger was that to me, a psychic invader who infiltrated my susceptible personality. It wasn't just the extraordinary state of his chaotic stacked properties collapsed into exhaustive ruin that burnt into me, it was more his singular focus on his reality being unquestionably the right one that impressed me so forcibly. His brain architecture like his crumbling real estate was submerged into a history that didn't include others. I learnt early that what we often call madness is simply an over-attachment to things that can't easily be shared, and so become obsessive. You meet a man of 77, when you're 19, totally fixated on his mummified mother, and everything proceeds from there in treating weird as normal. After that I made no effort to compromise, only to move further out from centre. And because poetry has so few readers, each one of them is worth a million; I got further into being a marginal. I've made a lifetime's career out of something that carries no social identity and little remuneration. It's a bit like being an astronaut manning an un-reusable rocket, only I don't need to return.

Why do poets take themselves so seriously when their work only reaches a few hundred people in a casual way? I've never cared about readers, my process is the adrenalin rush of writing, the dopamine bang in my cells. Why else write poetry if you don't get into altered chemistry. A should lead directly to Z and not B.

Psychedelic Meadow remains like a mirage to me, an excerpted hologram of dark green water, dense penumbral trees and whatever lurched perception writing and drugs created. What you see builds in the process of seeing by internal chemistry, and that's why none of us ever see the same thing, only a variant of what we imagine. Habituated Valium use, my drug, sometimes creates panic visuals – I see myself knocked over, injured, mugged, or collapsed on the pavement during rush hour as projected phenomenon. Sometimes I think it's really happened and pull out of the crowd into a side street.

I call it a tripped up way of seeing. In 1968 Chris Torrance published a floaty book of poetry *Green Orange Purple Red*, a sort of colour starting point for me with a jacket quote by Lee Harwood sitting on top of a Brighton cloud. It's funny how some things stick.

Bad Planet

A black rub inside the brain,
trapped in biology, force squeezes in
as bad planet, like licking a finger
on lemon drizzle, scratched like that
at mental patterns, sat there dipped
in a black coat, too-big sweater,
Electric Ladyland sleeve in your lap
like an imploded graffiti Shazam
in variform confusion – maybe you
saw me writing thirty years on
whatever you were feeling, gets like that
intuitively, a lost day
turns up again, like this crush in July
in a moon-coloured street in China Town
slung with red lanterns, still talking to you
with contents – what the poem does to fill
its local space like juice a ripe lemon.
I turn the corner; yellow light shoves through
so dusty it's like atmosphere samples,
or blown about hair, and I'm still with you
writing in writing that jumps 30 years.

Normandy Apple Fan

Rainless lightning; turbulent ultramarine churn
over the place we collected
sweet stuff like oozy purée –
apple given pop by lemon
in head-to-toe black she sold
what she made, green tea
lemonade from the back of time
like a sunglassed Mayan astronomer
chewing on an ochre dust cloud
400 light years away
facing in to us as quasi-tribal
valley weirdos – her Normandy genes
carved out of something like hot black tar
skewed towards the Asperger's end,
carrot pudding and onion quiche
amongst others her speciality
off a track you'd never track
to any purpose but retrieving sweet
adjectives and syrupy flan
doused in lemon juice written in brandy.

Normandy Apple Flan

Ingredients

12 oz short crusty pastry

I pint thick apple puree (sweetened)

3 dessert apples

Juice of two lemons

2 tablespoons apricot jam

2 tablespoons of water

Method

Line a 9" flan ring with the pastry and bake blind for 5-10 minutes. Fill the flan with the puree, peel and core sweet apples, cut into slices, and top the flan with the apples concentrically placed. Bake in a moderate oven for 20-30 minutes, remove and cool. Heat the jam, water and rest of the lemon until syrupy, do not allow to boil; press through a sieve and spoon over the tart to glaze.

Joan Woodhall *The Jersey Cook Book of St Helier*

Deeper

Our afternoons like roadmapping the brain's
information loops – parietal lobe
for spatial awareness, swipe buddleia,
a purple cone smelling of burnt honey
voluptuously wafting scent
and time like atoms stuck together
there on the road transparent as vodka
its window a parallel processed block
weightless as thought, a dreamy
indolent levitation we cut through
to a field called Mal y Tourne
describing its twisty boundaries, a place
we'd chill, shaping out our vision
like pointing ten years ahead at the sun
from our solar orange blanket,
our transient hold on local expired
each time we were chased off the bumpy land
down to the ferny ditch at Mont Misère,
immersed in our own, deeper the better,
carried on down to the hidden bottom.

Self-Help Manual

Writing poetry is a bit like operating in aerospace, a sort of quantum--quick repositioning of GBS into a freaky spatialization where travelling objects from different space-times intersect or don't. Do it long enough you don't know where you are, only you come back to words. They're all you've got like a Farrow and Ball colour chart to make your way in positioning. What's a word? The unit has far more potential value than any currency, money marketing, oil resource or space engineering, because its qualitative is instrumental to reinventing the universe. A single like can rephrase reality. That's what I get off on, the lawless remake of what's the scientifically accepted view of reality into imaginatively subverting it into unlimited alternatives. Fucking up systems with a scrunched fist of language.

And what's on the other side? All of those dead or instant snapshot friends that fill my poems, pick--ups, collusive strangers, weirdos, more what I've lost than gained. There's a poem of Thom Gunn's, 'I Love Elegy', about a friend who shoots himself under eucalyptus trees, and Gunn brings in the idea of total, and that there'll be no big reunion of friends round the bend in the river after death, and that it's only language provides the possibility of what can't otherwise happen. Writing poetry doesn't help right anything for me, it only makes loss more viewable through words. It compounds pain rather than modifies or releases it. The poem reinforces the irrevocable, and how language is really only like the film coating on a pill in terms of reaching hard experience. You can't really alter any state, you can only make it different. That's where poetry of a certain type comes in – it does something for the reader it can't do for the poet. It appears to make things better simply by altering the facts. Where does that get me personally? Nowhere and everywhere, sitting in a corner of the room, with an empty glass.

This is where distraction comes in, because writing bleeds into environment. I take mine OUT into cafes, public spaces, B-worlds, Soho village. It's there I dip back into Psych Meadow like sticking a drinking straw in a green smoothy. The ruined chalet comes up sunk in time and impudent waste with music crashing through the site. It's when I look up the densely treed hill back of the house I see Paula, and higher up Dave, just sitting there looking into the late afternoon light, busy contemplating the join between inner and outer geographies, that I'm closest to real.

All I can be sure of is that nobody else on Soho's Frith Street is seeing inwardly what I am. The two come down to meet me from the height and I've brought a bottle of wine for us to sink. It really happened, but poetry is my only way of telling and through it I'm the solitary messenger carrying news out of nowhere.

No Restart

October 31, you went away –
sunshine colours stored in your arteries,
a vascular rainbow, chill in the air
like plane metal at altitude,
tin-table rain, summer a blond chapter
reviewed like honey in a jar
put away to forget.
You left me books to sling on to a dream
Ed Dorn's *Gunslinger* – still got it
Julia and the Bazooka by guess who
some writings of your own snatched high
from psychoactive industry
still written into me – your clear vision
of mirage men come out the sun.
A time, no different to other times,
or say, orange to green, but it was ours
and ends up out of date, like everything
done or written, it's just me carries on
the story, blue or purple what's the difference
in fade, or mine or yours, the valley ends
in this twisted massive propulsive tree.

Clean

Five weeks without benzos, got benzo blues,
fog in my eyes, a scratchy throat,
hauling this poem up the atmosphere's curve
at Starbucks Belsize Park
like an orbital module – can't go back
so get what I can in real time
imagery rushes slammed with vitamins
like a Utah astronomer
getting a red win in the dark.
Writing's like watching people filing out
to board a plane in flashy
driving rain. There's no way back.
Those friends, they're sucked into the universe
as final, never to be the same again,
no acne pits as close identity,
no disappointment turned around to gain,
no little instant of a transient hope
taking on shine. No drug chasing my blood,
I get this clean, the way the biggest loss
weighs less than a sugar grain on a spoon.

Des Bourdelets

Ingredients

11 pounds shortcut pastry

6 large sweet apples

Method

Peel and core the apples. Roll out the pastry into rounds large enough to completely cover the apple, place one apple on each piece of pastry and wrap around the apple, tucking the ends into the core hole, place the fold side on the tray and bake in a moderate over 30-35 minutes.

CPSIA information can be obtained
at www.ICGtesting.com
Printed in the USA
BVHW071715220719
554055BV00009B/1065/P

9 781848 616271